IN MY HUMBLE
OPINION

KNOCK KNOCK®
VENICE, CALIFORNIA

Created and published by Knock Knock
Distributed by Who's There, Inc.
Venice, CA 90291
knockknockstuff.com

ISBN: 978-160106075-4
UPC: 825703-50021-9

10 9 8 7

OTHER PEOPLE ARE SO
ANNOYING

If it weren't for all those idiots, your life would be perfect. After all, you're a good driver, a sensible friend, a nuanced coworker, a caring mate, and, most of all, you know how to stand in a line without cutting. Given the antics of the thronging rabble, however, "If you're not angry, you're not paying attention," as the bumper sticker says. We'd probably all be better off if we *weren't* paying attention—to the tailgating jerk behind us, to the woman screeching into her cell phone, to the waiter who thinks he's God's gift. Two centuries before bumper stickers enriched our lives, the eighteenth-century poet Thomas Gray said "Ignorance is bliss," and no doubt it's still true.

For better or worse, you don't have the gift of oblivion. You notice every little irritating tic and injustice and spend your hours wondering why people are like that. And who could blame you? Plain and simple, there's a lot to vent about these days. Our concerns range from the significant (war, environmental destruction, the continued popularity of reality television) to smaller, everyday annoyances (stupid pop songs, telemarketers, and overpriced coffee) to the philosophical (do humans even *matter* in the cosmos?). You're paying attention, and the result is misanthropy ranging from the vague to the acute.

One justification for your aggravation level is the overcrowding of our contemporary world. We're living in congested cities, competing for resources, clogging highways, and generally rubbing up against one another. Supreme Court Justice Oliver Wendell Holmes Jr. famously stated, "The right to swing my fist ends where the other man's nose begins." The same could apply to loud music, cigarette smoke, and honking. The damaging effects of proximity have been proven: in renowned studies on the deliberate overcrowding of rats, high levels of aggression and compromised health were the inevitable result.

Annoyance isn't terribly good for you either. Research shows that those who score high on a hostility scale are substantially more likely to die earlier than those at low or average levels, primarily from heart disease. Physiologically, the effects of anger include the release of the hormones adrenaline and noradrenaline, increased heart rate and blood pressure, and the movement of sugar into the bloodstream. It also, however, appears to be something we crave—as much as sex, food, and drugs. According to a Vanderbilt University study, aggression engages the brain's reward pathways and involves dopamine.

We do seem to be delighted to compare our irritations with others—witness the blogging movement. In an article in the Minneapolis *Star Tribune*, Laura Lee, author of *The Pocket Encyclopedia of Aggravation*, notes, "People like hearing that other people are bugged by the same things" because "we're not stoning anyone or being killed by leeches, so we have that leisure to concentrate on petty annoyances." In his book *The Emotional Revolution*, Dr. Norman E. Rosenthal states, "Bad traffic, slow waiters, an insensitive boss, an incompetent employee, or an inattentive spouse are all common provocations."

But do you have to be angry to write down your humble opinions? Certainly not. "Humble opinion" is, of course, an understatement—whenever anybody uses that phrase, the presumption is that said opinion is correct and better than everyone else's. Even when it's expressed as an acronym online (IMHO), it's a false mitigation of what you know to be right—your view. And what better place to express that than a journal, where nobody can contradict you?

Whether you scribble your two cents' worth or vent your rage on any given day, journaling is a healthy outlet for your thoughts. You won't anger anybody else, and, should you be irritated, you might just work through your own anger. Experts now believe that anger is generally best when it's suppressed (not expressed) but that it can be damaging when it's repressed (not known or acknowledged). In his book *Anger: How to Recognize and Cope with It*, Dr. Leo Madow notes, "If anger is considered as 'energy,' it cannot be destroyed (forgotten) but must be converted."

Fortunately, the benefits of journal writing have been examined, to surprisingly consistent results. According to a widely cited study by James W. Pennebaker and Janel D. Seagal, "Writing about important personal experiences in an emotional way for as little as fifteen minutes over the course of three days brings about improvements in mental and physical health." Proven physical effects include stress management, strengthened immune systems, fewer doctor visits, and improvement in chronic illnesses such as asthma (clearly it's better to vent in your journal than to hyperventilate). "It's hard to believe," says Pennebaker, a psychology professor at the University of Texas at Austin, but "being able to put experiences into words is good for your physical health." Kathleen Adams, founder of the Center for Journal Therapy, calls journals "79-cent therapists."

It's not entirely clear how journaling accomplishes all this. The consensus among experts is that catharsis is involved, but they also point to the organization of experience into a narrative. According to *Newsweek*, some scholars believe that journaling "forces us to transform the ruminations cluttering our minds into coherent stories. Writing about an experience may also dull its emotional impact." Psychologist Ira Progoff, widely considered to be the father of the modern journaling movement, stated in 1975 that an "intensive journal process" could "draw each person's life toward wholeness at its own tempo."

As a devotee of this journal, you obviously have opinions, be they humble or (more likely) really smart. You've chosen not to blog (at least in this case) but rather to learn from your own conclusions and pet peeves. To best utilize the journaling process, however, don't blindly vent, as that may exacerbate your frustration with the teeming masses. Instead, get your feelings out, then try to understand them. A few additional tips to consider: experts agree that in order to reap the benefits of journaling, you have to stick with it, quasi-daily, for as little as five minutes at a time (at least fifteen minutes, however, is best). Finding regular writing times and comfortable locations can help with consistency. Prompt your writing with questions; in the case of this journal, elaborate on "Why people are like that today" and "Definitive conclusion about humanity." The *In My Humble Opinion* journal's quotations will also provide a jumping-off point for your writing. Renowned journaler Anaïs Nin suggests asking yourself, "What feels vivid, warm, or near to you at the moment?" Don't critique your writing as you journal; journaling is a process of self-reflection, not a constructed composition. In other words, spew. Finally, determine a home for your journal where others won't find it.

Thomas Jefferson declared, "When angry, count ten, before you speak. If very angry, an hundred." Mark Twain leavened Jefferson's advice: "When angry, count four. When very angry, swear." We say, "When you're angry, irritated, or you just have a humble opinion to express, journal."

Hell is other people.

JEAN-PAUL SARTRE

WHY PEOPLE ARE LIKE THAT TODAY:

_____
_____
_____
_____
_____
_____
_____
_____
_____
_____
_____
_____
_____
_____
_____
_____
_____
_____
_____
_____
_____
_____
_____
_____

TODAY'S DEFINITIVE CONCLUSION ABOUT HUMANITY:

I sometimes think that God in creating man somewhat overestimated his ability.

OSCAR WILDE

WHY PEOPLE ARE LIKE THAT TODAY:

_____

_____

_____

_____

_____

_____

_____

_____

_____

_____

_____

_____

_____

_____

_____

_____

_____

_____

_____

_____

_____

_____

_____

_____

_____

_____

_____

TODAY'S DEFINITIVE CONCLUSION ABOUT HUMANITY:

Human beings, who are almost unique
in having the ability to learn from the
experience of others, are also remarkable
for their apparent disinclination to do so.

DOUGLAS ADAMS

WHY PEOPLE ARE LIKE THAT TODAY:

The world is made up for the most part of morons and natural tyrants, sure of themselves, strong in their own opinions, never doubting anything.

CLARENCE DARROW

WHY PEOPLE ARE LIKE THAT TODAY:

_____

_____

_____

_____

_____

_____

_____

_____

_____

_____

_____

_____

_____

_____

_____

_____

_____

_____

_____

_____

_____

_____

_____

_____

_____

_____

_____

_____

_____

TODAY'S DEFINITIVE CONCLUSION ABOUT HUMANITY:

Only two things are infinite, the universe and human stupidity, and I'm not sure about the former.

ALBERT EINSTEIN

WHY PEOPLE ARE LIKE THAT TODAY:

_____

_____

_____

_____

_____

_____

_____

_____

_____

_____

_____

_____

_____

_____

_____

_____

_____

_____

_____

_____

_____

_____

_____

_____

_____

_____

_____

_____

_____

TODAY'S DEFINITIVE CONCLUSION ABOUT HUMANITY:

Many people would
sooner die than think.
In fact, they do.

BERTRAND RUSSELL

WHY PEOPLE ARE LIKE THAT TODAY:

_____

_____

_____

_____

_____

_____

_____

_____

_____

_____

_____

_____

_____

_____

_____

_____

_____

_____

_____

_____

_____

_____

_____

_____

_____

_____

_____

_____

TODAY'S DEFINITIVE CONCLUSION ABOUT HUMANITY:

Such is the human race. Often it does seem such a pity that Noah . . . didn't miss the boat.

MARK TWAIN

WHY PEOPLE ARE LIKE THAT TODAY:

TODAY'S DEFINITIVE CONCLUSION ABOUT HUMANITY:

And isn't your life extremely flat
with nothing whatever to grumble at!

———

W. S. GILBERT

WHY PEOPLE ARE LIKE THAT TODAY:

TODAY'S DEFINITIVE CONCLUSION ABOUT HUMANITY:

We must, however, acknowledge, as it seems to me, that man with all his noble qualities . . . still bears in his bodily frame the indelible stamp of his lowly origin.

CHARLES DARWIN

WHY PEOPLE ARE LIKE THAT TODAY:

_____

_____

_____

_____

_____

_____

_____

_____

_____

_____

_____

_____

_____

_____

_____

_____

_____

_____

_____

_____

_____

_____

_____

_____

_____

_____

_____

_____

TODAY'S DEFINITIVE CONCLUSION ABOUT HUMANITY:

The more humanity advances, the more it is degraded.

GUSTAVE FLAUBERT

WHY PEOPLE ARE LIKE THAT TODAY:

_____

_____

_____

_____

_____

_____

_____

_____

_____

_____

_____

_____

_____

_____

_____

_____

_____

_____

_____

_____

_____

_____

_____

_____

_____

_____

_____

TODAY'S DEFINITIVE CONCLUSION ABOUT HUMANITY:

Since I no longer expect
anything from mankind except
madness,
meanness, and mendacity;
egotism,
cowardice,
and
self-delusion,
I have stopped
being a
misanthrope.

IRVING LAYTON

DATE

WHY PEOPLE ARE LIKE THAT TODAY:

_____

_____

_____

_____

_____

_____

_____

_____

_____

_____

_____

_____

_____

_____

_____

_____

_____

_____

_____

_____

_____

_____

_____

_____

_____

TODAY'S DEFINITIVE CONCLUSION ABOUT HUMANITY:

The world is populated in the main
by people who should not exist.

GEORGE BERNARD SHAW

DATE

WHY PEOPLE ARE LIKE THAT TODAY:

_____
_____
_____
_____
_____
_____
_____
_____
_____
_____
_____
_____
_____
_____
_____
_____
_____
_____
_____
_____
_____
_____
_____
_____
_____
_____

TODAY'S DEFINITIVE CONCLUSION ABOUT HUMANITY:

I only go out to get
me a fresh appetite
for being alone.

LORD BYRON

WHY PEOPLE ARE LIKE THAT TODAY:

_____
_____
_____
_____
_____
_____
_____
_____
_____
_____
_____
_____
_____
_____
_____
_____
_____
_____
_____
_____
_____
_____
_____
_____
_____
_____
_____

TODAY'S DEFINITIVE CONCLUSION ABOUT HUMANITY:

The Bible tells us to love our neighbors, and also to love our enemies; probably because they are generally the same people.

G. K. CHESTERTON

DATE

WHY PEOPLE ARE LIKE THAT TODAY:

It's too bad that stupidity isn't painful.

ANTON LAVEY

WHY PEOPLE ARE LIKE THAT TODAY:

_____
_____
_____
_____
_____
_____
_____
_____
_____
_____
_____
_____
_____
_____
_____
_____
_____
_____
_____
_____
_____
_____
_____
_____

TODAY'S DEFINITIVE CONCLUSION ABOUT HUMANITY:

How I *hate* the attitude of ordinary people to life. How I loathe ordinariness! How from my soul I abhor nice simple people, with their eternal price list. It makes my blood boil.

D. H. LAWRENCE

WHY PEOPLE ARE LIKE THAT TODAY:

_____

_____

_____

_____

_____

_____

_____

_____

_____

_____

_____

_____

_____

_____

_____

_____

_____

_____

_____

_____

_____

_____

_____

_____

_____

_____

_____

_____

_____

_____

TODAY'S DEFINITIVE CONCLUSION ABOUT HUMANITY:

Everyone is as God made him, and often a great deal worse.

MIGUEL DE CERVANTES

DATE		

WHY PEOPLE ARE LIKE THAT TODAY:

_____

_____

_____

_____

_____

_____

_____

_____

_____

_____

_____

_____

_____

_____

_____

_____

_____

_____

_____

_____

_____

_____

_____

_____

_____

_____

_____

_____

_____

TODAY'S DEFINITIVE CONCLUSION ABOUT HUMANITY:

Some scientists claim that hydrogen, because it is so plentiful, is the basic building block of the universe. I dispute that. I say there is more stupidity than hydrogen, and that is the basic building block of the universe.

FRANK ZAPPA

DATE

WHY PEOPLE ARE LIKE THAT TODAY:

_____

_____

_____

_____

_____

_____

_____

_____

_____

_____

_____

_____

_____

_____

_____

_____

_____

_____

_____

_____

_____

_____

_____

_____

_____

TODAY'S DEFINITIVE CONCLUSION ABOUT HUMANITY:

The chief obstacle
to the progress of
the human race is
the human race.

——————

DON MARQUIS

DATE

WHY PEOPLE ARE LIKE THAT TODAY:

_____
_____
_____
_____
_____
_____
_____
_____
_____
_____
_____
_____
_____
_____
_____
_____
_____
_____
_____
_____
_____
_____
_____

TODAY'S DEFINITIVE CONCLUSION ABOUT HUMANITY:

In nature a repulsive caterpillar turns into a lovely butterfly. But with human beings it is the other way around: a lovely butterfly turns into a repulsive caterpillar.

ANTON CHEKHOV

DATE

WHY PEOPLE ARE LIKE THAT TODAY:

_____

_____

_____

_____

_____

_____

_____

_____

_____

_____

_____

_____

_____

_____

_____

_____

_____

_____

_____

_____

_____

_____

_____

TODAY'S DEFINITIVE CONCLUSION ABOUT HUMANITY:

Cynicism is an unpleasant way of saying the truth.

LILLIAN HELLMAN

WHY PEOPLE ARE LIKE THAT TODAY:

_____

_____

_____

_____

_____

_____

_____

_____

_____

_____

_____

_____

_____

_____

_____

_____

_____

_____

_____

_____

_____

_____

_____

TODAY'S DEFINITIVE CONCLUSION ABOUT HUMANITY:

Everyone looks retarded once you set your mind to it.

DAVID SEDARIS

DATE

WHY PEOPLE ARE LIKE THAT TODAY:

TODAY'S DEFINITIVE CONCLUSION ABOUT HUMANITY:

The only thing that will be remembered about my enemies after they're dead is the nasty things I've said about them.

CAMILLE PAGLIA

WHY PEOPLE ARE LIKE THAT TODAY:

_____

_____

_____

_____

_____

_____

_____

_____

_____

_____

_____

_____

_____

_____

_____

_____

_____

_____

_____

_____

_____

_____

_____

_____

TODAY'S DEFINITIVE CONCLUSION ABOUT HUMANITY:

I love humanity;
but I hate people.

EDNA ST. VINCENT MILLAY

DATE

WHY PEOPLE ARE LIKE THAT TODAY:

_____

_____

_____

_____

_____

_____

_____

_____

_____

_____

_____

_____

_____

_____

_____

_____

_____

_____

_____

_____

_____

_____

_____

_____

_____

_____

_____

TODAY'S DEFINITIVE CONCLUSION ABOUT HUMANITY:

Much virtue in herbs, little in men.

BENJAMIN FRANKLIN

WHY PEOPLE ARE LIKE THAT TODAY:

_____

_____

_____

_____

_____

_____

_____

_____

_____

_____

_____

_____

_____

_____

_____

_____

_____

_____

_____

_____

_____

_____

_____

TODAY'S DEFINITIVE CONCLUSION ABOUT HUMANITY:

The fundamental cause of trouble in the world today is that the stupid are cocksure while the intelligent are full of doubt.

BERTRAND RUSSELL

DATE		

WHY PEOPLE ARE LIKE THAT TODAY:

_____

_____

_____

_____

_____

_____

_____

_____

_____

_____

_____

_____

_____

_____

_____

_____

_____

_____

_____

_____

_____

_____

_____

_____

_____

_____

_____

_____

TODAY'S DEFINITIVE CONCLUSION ABOUT HUMANITY:

A true gentleman is one who is never unintentionally rude.

OSCAR WILDE

DATE

WHY PEOPLE ARE LIKE THAT TODAY:

_____
_____
_____
_____
_____
_____
_____
_____
_____
_____
_____
_____
_____
_____
_____
_____
_____
_____
_____
_____
_____
_____

TODAY'S DEFINITIVE CONCLUSION ABOUT HUMANITY:

When I think of the number of
disagreeable people that I know
who have gone to a better world, I
am sure hell won't be so bad at all.

MARK TWAIN

DATE		

WHY PEOPLE ARE LIKE THAT TODAY:

_____

_____

_____

_____

_____

_____

_____

_____

_____

_____

_____

_____

_____

_____

_____

_____

_____

_____

_____

_____

_____

_____

_____

_____

TODAY'S DEFINITIVE CONCLUSION ABOUT HUMANITY:

Don't overestimate the decency of the human race.

H. L. MENCKEN

WHY PEOPLE ARE LIKE THAT TODAY:

_____
_____
_____
_____
_____
_____
_____
_____
_____
_____
_____
_____
_____
_____
_____
_____
_____
_____
_____
_____
_____
_____
_____
_____
_____
_____
_____

TODAY'S DEFINITIVE CONCLUSION ABOUT HUMANITY:

Perhaps if we saw what was ahead of us, and glimpsed the crimes, follies, and misfortunes that would befall us later on, we would all stay in our mother's wombs, and then there would be nobody in the world but a great number of very fat, very irritated women.

———————

LEMONY SNICKET

WHY PEOPLE ARE LIKE THAT TODAY:

_____
_____
_____
_____
_____
_____
_____
_____
_____
_____
_____
_____
_____
_____
_____
_____
_____
_____
_____
_____
_____
_____
_____
_____
_____
_____
_____
_____
_____

TODAY'S DEFINITIVE CONCLUSION ABOUT HUMANITY:

Nobody ever lost a nickel betting against the intelligence of the American public.

P. T. BARNUM

DATE

WHY PEOPLE ARE LIKE THAT TODAY:

TODAY'S DEFINITIVE CONCLUSION ABOUT HUMANITY:

I don't have pet peeves, I have whole kennels of irritation.

WHOOPI GOLDBERG

WHY PEOPLE ARE LIKE THAT TODAY:

_____

_____

_____

_____

_____

_____

_____

_____

_____

_____

_____

_____

_____

_____

_____

_____

_____

_____

_____

_____

_____

_____

_____

_____

_____

TODAY'S DEFINITIVE CONCLUSION ABOUT HUMANITY:

The world is a prison in which solitary confinement is preferable.

KARL KRAUS

WHY PEOPLE ARE LIKE THAT TODAY:

TODAY'S DEFINITIVE CONCLUSION ABOUT HUMANITY:

If I could get my membership fee back, I'd resign from the human race.

FRED ALLEN

DATE		

WHY PEOPLE ARE LIKE THAT TODAY:

_____

_____

_____

_____

_____

_____

_____

_____

_____

_____

_____

_____

_____

_____

_____

_____

_____

_____

_____

_____

_____

_____

_____

_____

TODAY'S DEFINITIVE CONCLUSION ABOUT HUMANITY:

No man lives without
jostling and being jostled;
in all ways he has to elbow
himself through the world,
giving and receiving offense.

THOMAS CARLYLE

WHY PEOPLE ARE LIKE THAT TODAY:

TODAY'S DEFINITIVE CONCLUSION ABOUT HUMANITY:

Common sense is not so common.

VOLTAIRE

DATE		

WHY PEOPLE ARE LIKE THAT TODAY:

_____

_____

_____

_____

_____

_____

_____

_____

_____

_____

_____

_____

_____

_____

_____

_____

_____

_____

_____

_____

_____

_____

_____

_____

_____

_____

TODAY'S DEFINITIVE CONCLUSION ABOUT HUMANITY:

The nature of men and women—their essential nature—is so vile and despicable that if you were to portray a person as he really is, no one would believe you.

W. SOMERSET MAUGHAM

WHY PEOPLE ARE LIKE THAT TODAY:

_____
_____
_____
_____
_____
_____
_____
_____
_____
_____
_____
_____
_____
_____
_____
_____
_____
_____
_____
_____
_____
_____
_____
_____

TODAY'S DEFINITIVE CONCLUSION ABOUT HUMANITY:

The world is a botched job.

GABRIEL GARCÍA MÁRQUEZ

WHY PEOPLE ARE LIKE THAT TODAY:

_____
_____
_____
_____
_____
_____
_____
_____
_____
_____
_____
_____
_____
_____
_____
_____
_____
_____
_____
_____
_____
_____
_____
_____
_____

TODAY'S DEFINITIVE CONCLUSION ABOUT HUMANITY:

Optimism is the content of small men in high places.

F. SCOTT FITZGERALD

DATE

WHY PEOPLE ARE LIKE THAT TODAY:

_____
_____
_____
_____
_____
_____
_____
_____
_____
_____
_____
_____
_____
_____
_____
_____
_____
_____
_____
_____
_____
_____
_____
_____

TODAY'S DEFINITIVE CONCLUSION ABOUT HUMANITY:

Just think of how stupid the average person is, and then realize that half of them are even stupider.

GEORGE CARLIN

WHY PEOPLE ARE LIKE THAT TODAY:

_____

_____

_____

_____

_____

_____

_____

_____

_____

_____

_____

_____

_____

_____

_____

_____

_____

_____

_____

_____

_____

_____

_____

_____

TODAY'S DEFINITIVE CONCLUSION ABOUT HUMANITY:

Humanity is a pigsty, where liars, hypocrites, and the obscene in spirit congregate.

GEORGE MOORE

WHY PEOPLE ARE LIKE THAT TODAY:

TODAY'S DEFINITIVE CONCLUSION ABOUT HUMANITY:

I love mankind—it's people I can't stand.

CHARLES M. SCHULZ

DATE

WHY PEOPLE ARE LIKE THAT TODAY:

_____
_____
_____
_____
_____
_____
_____
_____
_____
_____
_____
_____
_____
_____
_____
_____
_____
_____
_____
_____
_____
_____
_____
_____
_____

TODAY'S DEFINITIVE CONCLUSION ABOUT HUMANITY:

You can get much further with a kind word and a gun than you can with a kind word alone.

AL CAPONE

DATE

WHY PEOPLE ARE LIKE THAT TODAY:

_____

_____

_____

_____

_____

_____

_____

_____

_____

_____

_____

_____

_____

_____

_____

_____

_____

_____

_____

_____

_____

_____

_____

_____

_____

TODAY'S DEFINITIVE CONCLUSION ABOUT HUMANITY:

Human beings cling to their
delicious tyrannies, and to their
exquisite nonsense . . . till death
stares them in the face.

_____

SYDNEY SMITH

DATE

WHY PEOPLE ARE LIKE THAT TODAY:

_____
_____
_____
_____
_____
_____
_____
_____
_____
_____
_____
_____
_____
_____
_____
_____
_____
_____
_____
_____
_____
_____
_____
_____
_____
_____
_____
_____

TODAY'S DEFINITIVE CONCLUSION ABOUT HUMANITY:

What can we know?
What are we all?
Poor silly half-brained
things peering out at
the infinite, with the
aspirations of angels
and the instincts
of beasts.

ARTHUR CONAN DOYLE

DATE

WHY PEOPLE ARE LIKE THAT TODAY:

_____
_____
_____
_____
_____
_____
_____
_____
_____
_____
_____
_____
_____
_____
_____
_____
_____
_____
_____
_____
_____
_____
_____
_____
_____
_____
_____
_____
_____
_____
_____

TODAY'S DEFINITIVE CONCLUSION ABOUT HUMANITY:

All men are intrinsical rascals, and I am only sorry that, not being a dog, I can't bite them.

LORD BYRON

WHY PEOPLE ARE LIKE THAT TODAY:

_____

_____

_____

_____

_____

_____

_____

_____

_____

_____

_____

_____

_____

_____

_____

_____

_____

_____

_____

_____

_____

_____

_____

_____

_____

_____

_____

TODAY'S DEFINITIVE CONCLUSION ABOUT HUMANITY:

I sometimes think of what future historians will say of us. A single sentence will suffice for modern man: he fornicated and read the papers.

_____

ALBERT CAMUS

WHY PEOPLE ARE LIKE THAT TODAY:

_____

_____

_____

_____

_____

_____

_____

_____

_____

_____

_____

_____

_____

_____

_____

_____

_____

_____

_____

_____

_____

_____

_____

_____

_____

_____

TODAY'S DEFINITIVE CONCLUSION ABOUT HUMANITY:

People think it must be fun to be a super genius, but they don't realize how hard it is to put up with all the idiots in the world.

BILL WATTERSON

WHY PEOPLE ARE LIKE THAT TODAY:

_____

_____

_____

_____

_____

_____

_____

_____

_____

_____

_____

_____

_____

_____

_____

_____

_____

_____

_____

_____

_____

_____

_____

_____

_____

_____

TODAY'S DEFINITIVE CONCLUSION ABOUT HUMANITY:

What wretched creature of what
    wretched kind,

Than man more weak, calamitous,
    and blind?

———

HOMER

WHY PEOPLE ARE LIKE THAT TODAY:

Cabbage, *n.*
A familiar
kitchen-garden
vegetable about
as large and wise
as a man's head.

AMBROSE BIERCE

WHY PEOPLE ARE LIKE THAT TODAY:

TODAY'S DEFINITIVE CONCLUSION ABOUT HUMANITY:

I personally think
we developed
language because
of our deep inner
need to complain.

LILY TOMLIN

WHY PEOPLE ARE LIKE THAT TODAY:

_____

_____

_____

_____

_____

_____

_____

_____

_____

_____

_____

_____

_____

_____

_____

_____

_____

_____

_____

_____

_____

_____

_____

_____

_____

_____

_____

_____

TODAY'S DEFINITIVE CONCLUSION ABOUT HUMANITY:

When they discover the center of the universe, a lot of people will be disappointed to discover they are not it.

BERNARD BAILEY

WHY PEOPLE ARE LIKE THAT TODAY:

_____
_____
_____
_____
_____
_____
_____
_____
_____
_____
_____
_____
_____
_____
_____
_____
_____
_____
_____
_____
_____
_____
_____
_____
_____
_____

TODAY'S DEFINITIVE CONCLUSION ABOUT HUMANITY:

Lord, what fools these mortals be!

WILLIAM SHAKESPEARE

DATE		

WHY PEOPLE ARE LIKE THAT TODAY:

_____

_____

_____

_____

_____

_____

_____

_____

_____

_____

_____

_____

_____

_____

_____

_____

_____

_____

_____

_____

_____

_____

_____

_____

TODAY'S DEFINITIVE CONCLUSION ABOUT HUMANITY:

The world is a stage, but
the play is badly cast.

———————

OSCAR WILDE

DATE		

WHY PEOPLE ARE LIKE THAT TODAY:

_____

_____

_____

_____

_____

_____

_____

_____

_____

_____

_____

_____

_____

_____

_____

_____

_____

_____

_____

_____

_____

_____

_____

_____

TODAY'S DEFINITIVE CONCLUSION ABOUT HUMANITY:

My loathings are
simple: stupidity,
oppression, crime,
cruelty, soft music.

VLADIMIR NABOKOV

DATE		

WHY PEOPLE ARE LIKE THAT TODAY:

_____

_____

_____

_____

_____

_____

_____

_____

_____

_____

_____

_____

_____

_____

_____

_____

_____

_____

_____

_____

_____

_____

_____

_____

_____

TODAY'S DEFINITIVE CONCLUSION ABOUT HUMANITY:

Man is a rational animal—
so at least I have been told.
Throughout a long life, I have
looked diligently for evidence
in favor of this statement, but
so far I have not had the good
fortune to come across it.

BERTRAND RUSSELL

WHY PEOPLE ARE LIKE THAT TODAY:

_____

_____

_____

_____

_____

_____

_____

_____

_____

_____

_____

_____

_____

_____

_____

_____

_____

_____

_____

_____

_____

_____

_____

_____

TODAY'S DEFINITIVE CONCLUSION ABOUT HUMANITY:

There are two sides
to every question:
my side and the
wrong side.

OSCAR LEVANT

WHY PEOPLE ARE LIKE THAT TODAY:

_____

_____

_____

_____

_____

_____

_____

_____

_____

_____

_____

_____

_____

_____

_____

_____

_____

_____

_____

_____

_____

_____

_____

_____

_____

_____

_____

_____

_____

_____

_____

_____

_____

TODAY'S DEFINITIVE CONCLUSION ABOUT HUMANITY:

When dealing with people, let us remember we are not dealing with creatures of logic. We are dealing with creatures of emotion, creatures bristling with prejudices and motivated by pride and vanity.

DALE CARNEGIE

WHY PEOPLE ARE LIKE THAT TODAY:

TODAY'S DEFINITIVE CONCLUSION ABOUT HUMANITY:

I am free of all prejudice. I hate everyone equally.

W. C. FIELDS

DATE

WHY PEOPLE ARE LIKE THAT TODAY:

_____
_____
_____
_____
_____
_____
_____
_____
_____
_____
_____
_____
_____
_____
_____
_____
_____
_____
_____
_____
_____
_____
_____
_____
_____
_____

TODAY'S DEFINITIVE CONCLUSION ABOUT HUMANITY:

Humanity i love you because
when you're hard up you pawn your
intelligence to buy a drink . . .

E. E. CUMMINGS

WHY PEOPLE ARE LIKE THAT TODAY:

TODAY'S DEFINITIVE CONCLUSION ABOUT HUMANITY:

The earth . . . has
a skin, and this skin
has diseases. One of
these diseases, for
example, is called
"man."

FRIEDRICH NIETZSCHE

DATE		

WHY PEOPLE ARE LIKE THAT TODAY:

_____

_____

_____

_____

_____

_____

_____

_____

_____

_____

_____

_____

_____

_____

_____

_____

_____

_____

_____

_____

_____

_____

_____

_____

_____

_____

TODAY'S DEFINITIVE CONCLUSION ABOUT HUMANITY:

Early in life I had to choose between honest arrogance and hypocritical humility. I chose the former and have seen no reason to change.

FRANK LLOYD WRIGHT

WHY PEOPLE ARE LIKE THAT TODAY:

_____
_____
_____
_____
_____
_____
_____
_____
_____
_____
_____
_____
_____
_____
_____
_____
_____
_____
_____
_____
_____
_____
_____
_____
_____
_____
_____

TODAY'S DEFINITIVE CONCLUSION ABOUT HUMANITY:

I regard you with
an indifference
closely bordering
on aversion.

ROBERT LOUIS STEVENSON

DATE

WHY PEOPLE ARE LIKE THAT TODAY:

TODAY'S DEFINITIVE CONCLUSION ABOUT HUMANITY:

God made everything out of nothing.
But the nothingness shows through.

PAUL VALÉRY

DATE

WHY PEOPLE ARE LIKE THAT TODAY:

_____
_____
_____
_____
_____
_____
_____
_____
_____
_____
_____
_____
_____
_____
_____
_____
_____
_____
_____
_____
_____
_____
_____
_____
_____
_____
_____
_____
_____

TODAY'S DEFINITIVE CONCLUSION ABOUT HUMANITY:

I've always been interested in
people, but I've never liked them.

———————————

W. SOMERSET MAUGHAM

DATE

WHY PEOPLE ARE LIKE THAT TODAY:

_____

_____

_____

_____

_____

_____

_____

_____

_____

_____

_____

_____

_____

_____

_____

_____

_____

_____

_____

_____

_____

_____

_____

_____

TODAY'S DEFINITIVE CONCLUSION ABOUT HUMANITY:

The power
of accurate
observation
is commonly
called cynicism
by those who
have not got it.

GEORGE BERNARD SHAW

WHY PEOPLE ARE LIKE THAT TODAY:

TODAY'S DEFINITIVE CONCLUSION ABOUT HUMANITY:

I like long walks,
especially when they
are taken by people
who annoy me.

FRED ALLEN

DATE

WHY PEOPLE ARE LIKE THAT TODAY:

_____
_____
_____
_____
_____
_____
_____
_____
_____
_____
_____
_____
_____
_____
_____
_____
_____
_____
_____
_____
_____
_____
_____
_____
_____
_____
_____
_____
_____
_____

TODAY'S DEFINITIVE CONCLUSION ABOUT HUMANITY:

I have never killed anyone, but I have read some obituary notices with great satisfaction.

CLARENCE DARROW

DATE		

WHY PEOPLE ARE LIKE THAT TODAY:

_____

_____

_____

_____

_____

_____

_____

_____

_____

_____

_____

_____

_____

_____

_____

_____

_____

_____

_____

_____

_____

_____

_____

TODAY'S DEFINITIVE CONCLUSION ABOUT HUMANITY:

Happiness in intelligent people
is the rarest thing I know.

ERNEST HEMINGWAY

WHY PEOPLE ARE LIKE THAT TODAY:

TODAY'S DEFINITIVE CONCLUSION ABOUT HUMANITY:

We are all worms.
But I do believe that
I am a glow-worm.

WINSTON CHURCHILL

DATE

WHY PEOPLE ARE LIKE THAT TODAY:

_____
_____
_____
_____
_____
_____
_____
_____
_____
_____
_____
_____
_____
_____
_____
_____
_____
_____
_____
_____
_____
_____
_____
_____
_____
_____
_____

TODAY'S DEFINITIVE CONCLUSION ABOUT HUMANITY:

That's how it is on this bitch of an earth.

SAMUEL BECKETT

DATE

WHY PEOPLE ARE LIKE THAT TODAY:

TODAY'S DEFINITIVE CONCLUSION ABOUT HUMANITY:

Man was made at the end of the week's work, when God was tired.

MARK TWAIN

DATE

WHY PEOPLE ARE LIKE THAT TODAY:

_____

_____

_____

_____

_____

_____

_____

_____

_____

_____

_____

_____

_____

_____

_____

_____

_____

_____

_____

_____

_____

_____

_____

_____

_____

TODAY'S DEFINITIVE CONCLUSION ABOUT HUMANITY:

I prefer rogues to imbeciles, because they sometimes take a rest.

ALEXANDRE DUMAS, PÈRE

DATE

WHY PEOPLE ARE LIKE THAT TODAY:

TODAY'S DEFINITIVE CONCLUSION ABOUT HUMANITY:

There are few people whom I really love, and still fewer of whom I think well. The more I see of the world, the more am I dissatisfied with it; and every day confirms my belief of the inconsistency of all human characters, and of the little dependence that can be placed on the appearance of merit or sense.

JANE AUSTEN

DATE

WHY PEOPLE ARE LIKE THAT TODAY:

_____

_____

_____

_____

_____

_____

_____

_____

_____

_____

_____

_____

_____

_____

_____

_____

_____

_____

_____

_____

_____

_____

_____

_____

_____

_____

_____

_____

_____

TODAY'S DEFINITIVE CONCLUSION ABOUT HUMANITY:

I think everybody's nuts.

JOHNNY DEPP

DATE

WHY PEOPLE ARE LIKE THAT TODAY:

_____
_____
_____
_____
_____
_____
_____
_____
_____
_____
_____
_____
_____
_____
_____
_____
_____
_____
_____
_____
_____
_____
_____
_____
_____
_____
_____
_____

TODAY'S DEFINITIVE CONCLUSION ABOUT HUMANITY:

Maybe this world is another planet's hell.

ALDOUS HUXLEY

DATE

WHY PEOPLE ARE LIKE THAT TODAY:

_____

_____

_____

_____

_____

_____

_____

_____

_____

_____

_____

_____

_____

_____

_____

_____

_____

_____

_____

_____

_____

_____

_____

_____

_____

_____

_____

_____

_____

_____

_____

TODAY'S DEFINITIVE CONCLUSION ABOUT HUMANITY:

It's hard to be
humble when
you're as great
as I am.

_____

MUHAMMAD ALI

WHY PEOPLE ARE LIKE THAT TODAY:

_____

_____

_____

_____

_____

_____

_____

_____

_____

_____

_____

_____

_____

_____

_____

_____

_____

_____

_____

_____

_____

_____

_____

_____

_____

_____

TODAY'S DEFINITIVE CONCLUSION ABOUT HUMANITY:

So there.

KNOCK KNOCK